Time-Savers for Teachers

SPELLING YEARS 3-4

Peter Clutterbuck

FRANKLIN WATTS
LONDON•SYDNEY

How to use this book

This book provides a range of worksheets suitable for children in Years 3 and 4 of primary school. The worksheets are grouped into sections that correspond to the word level work specified in the National Literacy Strategy. The contents are equally relevant to the Scottish 5–14 Guidelines, and the curricula for the Republic and Northern Ireland.

Each section starts with an *introduction* that sets the topic in context. The worksheets that follow cater for *different* levels of ability. Complete *answers* are provided to save time with marking. You can then keep the worksheets as part of the pupils' *assessment* records.

All teacher-pages have a vertical stripe down the side of the page. All the worksheets are photocopiable.

This edition first published in 2004

Franklin Watts
338 Euston Road, London NW1 3BH

UK adaptation by Brenda Stones
Educational advisers: Sarah St John, Jo Owston

This edition not for sale outside the United Kingdom and Eire

ISBN 978 0 7496 5802 1

Printed in Dubai

Franklin Watts is a division of Hachette Children's Books.

Contents

Medium frequency words to be taught through Year 4

National Literacy Strategy Framework

Year 4
Term 1:

ask(ed), began, being, brought, can't, change, coming, didn't, does, don't, found, goes, gone, heard, I'm, jumped, knew, know, leave, might, opened, show, started, stopped, think, thought, told, tries, turn(ed), used, walk(ed)(ing), watch, woke(n), write.

Term 2:

almost, always, any, before, better, during, every, first, half, morning, much, never, number, often, only, second, sometimes, still, suddenly, today, until, upon, while, year, young.

Term 3:

above, across, along, also, around, below, between, both, different, follow(ing), high, inside, near, other, outside, place, right, round, such, through, together, under, where, without.

The complete list for Years 4–5

above	don't	morning	think
across	during	mother	those
almost	earth	much	thought
along	every	near	through
also	eyes	never	today
always	father	number	together
animal	first	often	told
any	follow(ing)	only	tries
around	found	opened	turn(ed)
asked	friends	other	under
baby	garden	outside	until
balloon	goes	own	upon
before	gone	paper	used
began	great	place	walk(ed)(ing)
being	half	right	watch
below	happy	round	where
better	head	second	while
between	heard	show	white
birthday	high	sister	whole
both	I'm	small	why
brother	important	something	window
brought	inside	sometimes	without
can't	jumped	sound	woke(n)
change	knew	started	word
children	know	still	work
clothes	lady	stopped	world
coming	leave	such	write
didn't	light	suddenly	year
different	might	sure	young
does	money	swimming	

Introduction to Onset and Rime

In the teaching material on phonological awareness at Key Stage 1, it was reckoned that by splitting a word into its initial consonant sound (the 'onset') and the vowel and final consonant sound (the 'rime'), children were best helped to distinguish the rhyming part of the word from the initial letter sound.

This section therefore revises that practice from Key Stage 1, using onsets of either a single consonant or a consonant cluster, and rimes with either a short vowel or long vowel phoneme.

Teachers should find that this reinforces children's awareness of sound patterns and regular spelling rules, and helps them spell new words by analogy with those they already know.

However, attention should also be drawn to words that share common spelling patterns but are sounded differently, e.g. ear, ead.

Onset and Rime

Name _____

Join the letter groups to make a word that matches the picture.

a. f + ish

= [   ]

b. pl + ant

= [   ]

c. br + ick

= [   ]

d. cr + ayon

= [   ]

e. dr + ess

= [   ]

f. pl + um

= [   ]

g. w + atch

= [   ]

h. cl + oud

= [   ]

i. dr + agon

= [   ]

j. sn + ail

= [   ]

k. sk + ate

= [   ]

l. cl + imb

= [   ]

m. sn + ake

= [   ]

n. w + olf

= [   ]

o. sh + eet

= [   ]

Onset and Rime

Name _____

1. **Add a letter string to make a word that matches the picture.**

Use these letter strings.

air	amp	are	ate
ain	ape	art	ale

a. gr**ape**___   **b.** ch_____   **c.** t_____   **d.** h_____

e. st_____   **f.** l_____   **g.** wh_____   **h.** sk_____

2. **Add a letter string to make a word that matches the picture.**

Use these letter strings.

eer	ent	ess	eal
ell	est	eep	eat

a. n_____   **b.** dr_____   **c.** t_____   **d.** s_____

e. d_____   **f.** b_____   **g.** w_____   **h.** s_____

3. **Make two rhyming words.**

a. t
   [ie] _____
   p   _____

b. f
   [ive] _____
   h   _____

c. c
   [oat] _____
   b   _____

Onset and Rime

Name _____

1. **Make a word to match the picture.**

    Use these letter strings.

ear	eep	ent	eak
atch	ick	ire	ive

    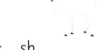

    a. b_____   b. t_____   c. sh_____   d. b_____

    e. m_____   f. br_____   g. f_____   h. h_____

2. **Complete each word group.**

    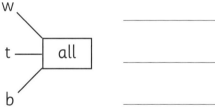

    a. w
        t — all
        b
        _____
        _____
        _____

    b. h
        f — ill
        g
        _____
        _____
        _____

    c. d
        m — ice
        r
        _____
        _____
        _____

    d. p
        b — ear
        w
        _____
        _____
        _____

3. **Write the letter string common to each group. The first one has been done for you.**

    a. deep keep peep **eep**   e. tape grape shape _____

    b. bend mend send _____   f. farm warm harm _____

    c. dear fear bear _____   g. bash wash smash _____

    d. weak peak beak _____   h. bask cask flask _____

Onset and Rime

Name _____

1. Write each word under the letter string it contains.

space	black	race	table
page	wage	stable	sack

a. able   **b.** age   **c.** ack   **d.** ace

_____   _____   _____   _____

_____   _____   _____   _____

2. Add a letter string to make a word that matches the picture.

able	air	ake	ain
all	ail	and	air

a. sn_____   **b.** t_____   **c.** ch_____   **d.** ch_____

e. w_____   **f.** c_____   **g.** h_____   **h.** h_____

3. Circle the two words in each group that have the same letter string.

a. tale sale wall	**e.** farm warm cape
b. tall pair hair	**f.** gas cart dart
c. hang lame sang	**g.** rash task flask
d. chain lake fake	**h.** hear train dear

Onset and Rime

Name _____

1. **Make words to match the pictures. Use a word part from Box A and Box B.**

BOX A		
d	s	f
p	t	b

BOX B		
eak	ear	arm
eal	art	eer

a. _____   b. _____   c. _____   d. _____

e. _____   f. _____   g. _____   h. _____

2.

ape	tart	mask	sheep
shell	raw	bread	glass

Which word

a. is used to make windows? _____

b. is a small cake? _____

c. is a type of primate? _____

d. is an animal that gives us wool? _____

e. is a food made from flour? _____

f. does a snail have? _____

g. means not cooked? _____

h. is something we wear over our faces? _____

3. **Can you spot six words in the box? Use them to complete the sentences.**

weststewcoldboatstoneboil

a. The hot water began to _____.

b. We went east then turned _____.

c. In summer it is hot but in winter it is _____.

d. I threw a _____ into the river.

e. I ate a _____ for tea last night.

f. We rowed the _____ across the lake.

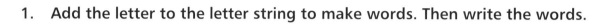

Onset and Rime

Name _____

1. Add the letter to the letter string to make words. Then write the words.

a. r
f — [ace]
sp

_____
_____
_____

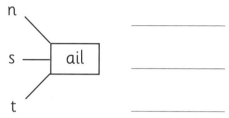

b. n
s — [ail]
t

_____
_____
_____

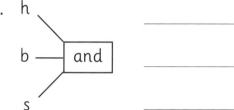

c. h
b — [and]
s

_____
_____
_____

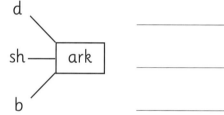

d. d
sh — [ark]
b

_____
_____
_____

2. Add a letter string to make words that match the pictures.

| ear | atch | aw |
| ice | itch | ight |

a. p_____

b. cl_____

c. d_____

d. w_____

e. w_____

f. l_____

3. Choose the correct letter string to complete each word.

a. h_____ (ave ive)

b. br_____ (ack ick)

c. pl_____ (ow ate)

d. w_____ (ind and)

e. gr_____ (ass ab)

f. b_____ (ath oth)

Onset and Rime

Name _____

1. **Use each word to complete a sentence.**

   Words with the **own** letter string.

frown	drown	flown	known
grown	gown	sown	town

   a. The small seedling has _____ into a large tree.

   b. The lady wore a blue _____ to the ball.

   c. Sandra is a well _____ actor on television.

   d. When we arrived at the nest the bird had _____ away.

   e. The farmer has now _____ his crops for this season.

   f. Our teacher began to _____ when we didn't know the answer.

   g. The small child was lucky not to _____ in the deep water.

   h. On our journey we passed through a small _____ .

2. **Add a word that contains the same letter string.**

sound	dome	shove	born
gloss	ghost	store	cartoon

   a. corner   morning   **born**

   b. nostril   frost   _____

   c. moss   across   _____

   d. home   gnome   _____

   e. ground   found   _____

   f. explore   score   _____

   g. harpoon   balloon   _____

   h. cove   move   _____

3. **Add a letter string to complete each word.**

   Use these letter strings.

oon	ong	ice	ove
oat	ound	ose	ief

   a. r_____ (a grain)

   b. thr_____ (part of your body)

   c. wr_____ (not correct)

   d. b_____ (tied up with rope)

   e. bab_____ (large monkey)

   f. br_____ (short, to the point)

   g. d_____ (amount of medicine)

   h. sh_____ (to push)

Onset and Rime

Name _____

1. Write each word under its letter string.

wind	blind	nest	home
come	catch	some	west
test	watch	match	find

a. ome

b. ind

c. est

d. atch

_____ _____ _____ _____

_____ _____ _____ _____

_____ _____ _____ _____

2. Write the letter string that is common to each group of words.

a. mate plate water _____

b. reach teach peach _____

c. shout about scout _____

d. zone cone alone _____

e. coat boat throat _____

f. swift fifty shift _____

g. roar soar boar _____

h. core tore store _____

i. quick thick brick _____

j. pass grass glass _____

3. Add a letter string to complete each word.

Use these letter strings.

oat	air	ake	ark
one	ive	one	own

a. c_____ (something we eat)

b. h_____ (a bee's home)

c. sh_____ (large fish)

d. h_____y (bees make it)

e. g_____ (an animal that butts)

f. br_____ (a colour)

g. b_____ (dogs chew them)

h. ch_____ (we sit on it)

Onset and Rime

Name _____

1. **Join a letter from Box A to a pattern from Box B to make words.**

BOX A			
p	h	t	n
h	s	p	b

BOX B			
ive	oes	est	ome
ell	eat	each	ork

a. meat of a pig _____

b. where you live _____

c. home of a bird _____

d. something that rings _____

e. part of your feet _____

f. home of a bee _____

g. something to sit on _____

h. a fruit _____

2. **Find words in the grid. Then complete each sentence.**

c	a	k	e	p
b	r	m	w	a
a	a	a	a	p
l	n	i	l	e
l	g	l	l	r

a. You can bounce a _____.

b. Pages are made of _____.

c. I _____ the bell at twelve o'clock.

d. Humpty Dumpty sat on a _____.

e. I ate a _____ for my lunch.

f. I got three letters in the _____.

3. **Write each word under its letter string.**

| bare | date | want | gas | care |
| task | past | fast | plate | plant |

a. ant   **b.** are   **c.** as   **d.** ate   **e.** ast

_____   _____   _____   _____   _____

_____   _____   _____   _____   _____

Onset and Rime

Name _____

1. **Complete each sentence.**

   Use these words.

bird	third	first	dirty
thirsty	shirt	birthday	stir

   a. After I put sugar in my tea I began to _____ it.

   b. The _____ flew to its nest in the tall tree.

   c. After the long run in the park I felt _____.

   d. Mike wore a blue cotton _____ to school.

   e. Today is Asha's seventh _____.

   f. The girl who came _____ won the race.

   g. Tom is in the fifth year but Sally is in the _____ year.

   h. We washed the _____ clothes at the laundrette.

2. **Circle the word that does not contain the same letter string.**

   a. witch   stitch   ditch   wire   **e.** ride   gift   hide   wide

   b. move   sift   drift   shift   **f.** five   give   lift   hive

   c. chew   bird   flew   drew   **g.** does   book   shoes   toes

   d. west   pest   nest   some   **h.** dome   cone   home   come

3. **Complete each word to match the picture.**

   Use these letter strings.

own	oat	old	oes	oast
ork	ose	ust	ull	

   a. cr_____   **b.** g_____   **c.** t_____

   d. g_____   **e.** d_____   **f.** f_____

   g. sh_____   **h.** b_____   **i.** r_____

Onset and Rime

Name _____

1. **Write the letter string common to each group.**

   a. beak leak weak peak _____

   b. keep peep sweep deep _____

   c. cheer deer steer beer _____

   d. cell spell sell fell _____

   e. bend send spend friend _____

   f. bent scent sent went _____

   g. tide ride side hide _____

   h. bake cake take lake _____

2. **Make each word match the picture.**

   Use these letter strings.

ark	ate	each	atch
ath	ice	ie	ire

   a. b_____

   b. sh_____

   c. m_____

   d. p_____

   e. f_____

   f. t_____

   g. m_____

   h. g_____

3. **Find words in the grid that have these patterns.**

h	h	r	f	w	n
i	i	i	i	i	e
l	d	d	l	r	s
l	e	e	l	e	t
f	i	r	e	x	x
b	e	s	t	c	y

   ide _____ _____

   ire _____ _____

   ill _____ _____

   est _____ _____

Onset and Rime

Name _____

1. **Complete each word.**

   Use these letter strings.

ear	oke	ack	ain
ate	one	ass	ead

   a. sm_____ (a fire gives it off)

   b. w_____r (we drink it)

   c. gl_____ (found in a window)

   d. tr_____ (a pathway)

   e. y_____ (twelve months)

   f. st_____ (a rock)

   g. br_____ (food made from flour)

   h. ch_____ (links of metal)

2. **Add the correct vowel pair to make a word.**

   a. sh_____t (oi ou) to yell loudly

   b. ch_____n (ei ai) links of metal

   c. m_____t (ea ai) flesh of animals

   d. qu_____t (ie ei) noiseless

   e. s_____p (oa ai) we wash with it

   f. h_____r (ai au) grows on your head

   g. s_____th (ie ou) a direction

   h. r_____nd (ou au) circular

3. **Words do not have to look the same to sound the same. Write each word beside the word that rhymes.**

June	hair	near	stood
shoe	wash	much	sail

   a. male _____

   b. blue _____

   c. deer _____

   d. touch _____

   e. fare _____

   f. gosh _____

   g. soon _____

   h. would _____

Onset and Rime

Name _____

1.  **Add a word which contains the same letter string.**

Use these.

stable	race	shade	~~stage~~
paid	sail	hair	cake

a. page wage rage **stage**

e. chair stair fair _____

b. snail trail fail _____

f. take bake mistake _____

c. maid said afraid _____

g. cable fable table _____

d. space face lace _____

h. blade made fade _____

2. **Choose the correct letter pattern to complete each word.**

(ife   ave)

a. kn_____

(itch   atch)

b. w_____

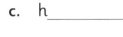

(ave   ive)

c. h_____

(old   one)

d. b_____

(are   ore)

e. st_____

(irt   ort)

f. sh_____

3. **Write the letter string each word contains. The first one has been done for you.**

a. horn   born   corn **orn**

e. gull   pull   full _____

b. fork   stork   cork _____

f. cross   gloss   floss _____

c. maid   said   afraid _____

g. work   pork   fork _____

d. space   face   lace _____

h. dust   gust   crust _____

Answers to Onset and Rime

Answers to page 7

fish, plant, brick, crayon, dress, plum, watch, cloud, dragon, snail, skate, climb, snake, wolf, sheet

Answers to page 8

1 chair, tart, hare, stair, lamp, whale, skate

2 nest, dress, tent, seal, deer, bell, weep, seat

3 tie, pie; five, hive; coat, boat

Answers to page 9

1 bear, tent, sheep, beak, match, brick, fire, hive

2 wall, tall, ball; hill, fill, gill; dice, mice, rice; pear, bear, wear

3 end, ear, eak, ape, arm, ash, ask

Answers to page 10

1 able, table, stable; age, page, wage; ack, black, sack; ace, space, race

2 snail, table, chair, chain, wall, cake, hand, hair

3 tale, sale; pair, hair; hang, sang; lake, fake; farm, warm; cart, dart; task, flask; hear, dear

Answers to page 11

1 deer, farm, dart, seal, peak, beak, bear, tear

2 glass, tart, ape, sheep, bread, shell, raw, mask

3 boil, west, cold, stone, stew, boat

Answers to page 12

1 race, face, space; nail, sail, tail; hand, band, sand; dark, shark, bark

2 pear, claw, dice, witch, watch, light

3 hive, brick, plate, wand, grass, bath

Answers to page 13

1 grown, gown, known, flown, sown, frown, drown, town

2 born, ghost, gloss, dome, sound, store, cartoon, shove

3 rice, throat, wrong, bound, baboon, brief, dose, shove

Answers to page 14

1 come, some, home; wind, blind, find; test, nest, west; catch, watch, match

2 ate, each, out, one, oat, ift, oar, ore, ick, ass

3 cake, hive, shark, honey, goat, brown, bone, chair

Answers to page 15

1 pork, home, nest, bell, toes, hive, seat, peach

2 ball, paper, rang, wall, cake, mail

3 want, plant; bare, care; gas, task; date, plate; past, fast

Answers to page 16

1 stir, bird, thirsty, shirt, birthday, first, third, dirty

2 wire, move, bird, some, gift, lift, book, cone

3 crown, goat, toast, gold, dust, fork, shoes, bull, rose

Answers to page 17

1 eak, eep, eer, ell, end, ent, ide, ake

2 bath, shark, mice, peach, fire, tie, match, gate

3 hide, ride; wire, fire; hill, fill; nest, best

Answers to page 18

1 smoke, water, glass, track, year, stone, bread, chain

2 shout, chain, meat, quiet, soap, hair, south, round

3 sail, shoe, near, much, hair, wash, June, stood

Answers to page 19

1 sail, paid, race, hair, cake, stable, shade

2 knife, watch, hive, bone, store, shirt

3 ork, aid, ace, ull, oss, ork, ust

Introduction to Consonant Clusters

This is also a revision of work first taught in Year 1, but well worth practising through Years 3 and 4.

Most of the sheets are on initial clusters, therefore similar to the practice of onset and rime, but the later worksheets then revise end clusters too.

The final sheet introduces the ending -ight, which is listed throughout the National Literacy Strategy for Years 3 and 4: 'spelling by analogy with other known words, e.g. light, fright'.

Note also that consonant clusters may be called blends, i.e. beginning blends or final blends.

Consonant Clusters

Name _____

Write the beginning blend or letter below each picture. Add them together to make a word. The first one has been done for you.

a.

| sh | + | a | + | d | + | e | = | shade |

b.

☐ + ☐ + ☐ + ☐ = ☐

c.

☐ + ☐ + ☐ + ☐ = ☐

d.

☐ + ☐ + ☐ + ☐ = ☐

e.

☐ + ☐ + ☐ + ☐ = ☐

f.

☐ + ☐ + ☐ + ☐ = ☐

22

Consonant Clusters

Name _____

1. **Add the correct piece to complete each word.**

a.
| br |
| ead |
| fl |
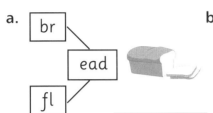
_____

b.
| cl |
| icket |
| cr |
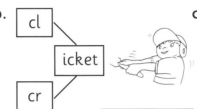
_____

c.
| br |
| idle |
| bl |
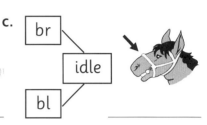
_____

d.
| cr |
| adle |
| dr |
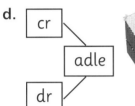
_____

e.
| fr |
| ower |
| fl |
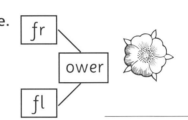
_____

f.
| pl |
| ate |
| pr |
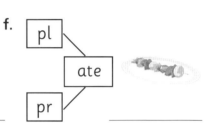
_____

2. **Write each word below the correct picture.**

| storm | straw | stamp | stove |
| stairs | sting | stir | stream |

a. _____   b. _____   c. _____   d. _____

e. _____   f. _____   g. _____   h. _____

3. **Colour tr words red, sp words blue, and sc words green.**

trunk	scrap	scar	scarf	school
scooter	tractor	trail	sponge	spark
track	spent	speak	trick	treat
spine	spoil	scout	spring	score
scrub	triangle	spray	train	tramp

Consonant Clusters

Name _____

1. **Colour red all living things. Colour blue all non-living things.**

crocodile	shore	swan
truck	snail	plate
sparrow	stain	snake
spade	spider	bread

2. **Colour blue all the things that you can eat.**
   Colour red all the things you can wear.

plum	scarf	gravy
skirt	bread	slipper
trousers	glove	glasses
fruit	scone	spinach

3. **Can you spot all the words in this jumble?**

sparrowspearspadespinespringsport

Which word

a. is a weapon? _____

b. is a game? _____

c. is a garden tool? _____

d. is a season? _____

e. is a bird? _____

f. is part of your back? _____

Consonant Clusters

Name _____

1. **Add the correct blend to complete each word.**

sw	pl	tr	sk	sc	sl

a. _____ug    b. _____iangle   c. _____im

d. _____rew   e. _____edge   f. _____ipping

2. **Draw a line from the picture to the correct word.**

a. tractor

truck

b. globe

glow

c. planet

plum

d. grease

greet

e. slipper

sleeve

f. scout

scone

3. **Write these tw words in their correct pattern.**

twitch	twice	twig	twenty	twelve	twin

a.   b.    c.

d.    e.    f.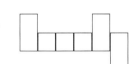

Consonant Clusters

Name _____

1. Write each **cr** word below the correct picture.

crocodile   crane   crown   cross
crawl   cricket   crust   cradle

a. _____   b. _____   c. _____   d. _____

e. _____   f. _____   g. _____   h. _____

2. Write each **st** word below its picture.

string   stable   straight   stitch
story   stone   stump   steak

a. _____   b. _____   c. _____   d. _____

e. _____   f. _____   g. _____   h. _____

3. Write the words in pairs by matching up their starting letters.

green   freckle   pretty   smile
smack   prince   fresh   grin

_____ _____

_____ _____

Consonant Clusters

Name _____

1. Add a blend to complete each word.

gr	sp	sn	sp
pl	br	cl	cr

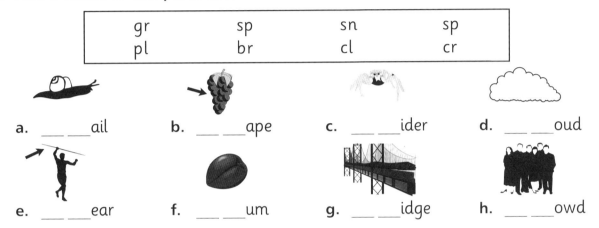

a. _____ail

b. _____ape

c. _____ider

d. _____oud

e. _____ear

f. _____um

g. _____idge

h. _____owd

2. Draw a line from the correct word to the picture.

a. breath
   bread

b. cliff
   click

c. flour
   flower

d. crown
   crowd

e. plum
   plump

f. globe
   glove

g. smoke
   smile

h. scone
   scorn

i. snail
   snake

j. spire
   splinter

k. triangle
   treasure

l. swan
   swap

3. Add the correct piece to complete each word.

a. tr / actor / sw _____
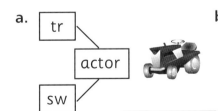

b. sp / arrow / st _____
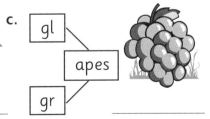

c. gl / apes / gr _____

d. pl / anet / pr _____
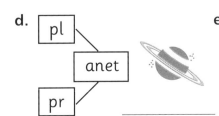

e. br / anch / bl _____
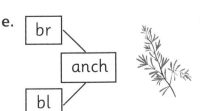

f. fl / ute / fr _____
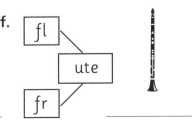

Consonant Clusters

Name _____

1. **Draw a ring around all the fl words in the grid. Then write them beside their meanings.**

f	l	e	a	f	f	f
f	f	f	f	l	l	l
l	l	l	l	o	o	e
o	o	a	u	c	o	e
u	o	m	t	k	r	t
r	d	e	e	x	x	x

a. too much water _____

b. part of a fire _____

c. group of sheep _____

d. musical instrument _____

e. a sucking insect _____

f. large group of warships _____

g. food made from wheat _____

h. part of a house _____

2. **Use br, bl or pr to complete each word.**

a. ___ ___ind (unable to see)

b. ___ ___idle (leather strap to guide a horse)

c. ___ ___iest (holy person)

d. ___ ___ain (organ of the body)

e. ___ ___ood (fluid of the body)

f. ___ ___ison (where criminals are sent)

g. ___ ___anket (bed covering)

h. ___ ___anch (limb of a tree)

3. **Unjumble the letters to make a word that matches the picture.**

a. leeps _____

b. nakes _____

c. idresp _____

d. lgass _____

e. gnair _____

f. lupm _____

Consonant Clusters

Name _____

1. **Write the words in pairs by matching up their starting letters.**

| slave | snare | sledge | cliff |
| climb | scar | scrap | sneeze |

_____   _____   _____   _____

_____   _____   _____   _____

2. **Add the correct letters to begin each word.**

a. ___ ___edge
(sl st)

b. ___ ___ire
(sn sp)

c. ___ ___ate
(sk sp)

d. ___ ___iff
(cl cr)

e. ___ ___eak
(sl st)

f. ___ ___allow
(sw st)

3. **Rearrange the letters to make a word that fits the definition.**

a. swap (an insect) _____

b. stew (a direction) _____

c. steal (stories) _____

d. span (cooking pots) _____

e. slip (part of your mouth) _____

f. scar (vehicles) _____

g. sport (where ships unload) _____

h. slog (pieces of wood) _____

Consonant Clusters

Name _____

1. **Find words in the grid. Write them in pairs under their starting letters.**

t	s	m	o	k	e	s	s
r	s	t	r	a	w	l	l
u	t	w	i	c	e	a	i
y	s	t	u	m	p	y	p
y	t	r	a	c	k	f	f
t	w	e	l	v	e	l	l
s	m	o	o	t	h	e	y
t	r	s	m	z	x	a	x

tw _____ st _____

_____ _____

sm _____ tr _____

_____ _____

sl _____ fl _____

_____ _____

2. **Each of these words begins with br.**

bread	bridge	breakfast	broad
branch	bridle	brook	bright

Which word means

a. wide? _____

b. a span over a river? _____

c. the first meal of the day? _____

d. a food made from flour? _____

e. part of a tree? _____

f. leather harness to control a horse? _____

3. **Complete each word.**

Use these blends.

pr	cr	fl	pl
gr	cl	bl	sp

a. ___ ___ocodile (a large reptile)

b. _ ___ea (a small sucking insect)

c. ___ ___um (a small fruit)

d. ___ ___esent (a gift)

e. ___ ___in (a cheeky smile)

f. ___ ___ean (not dirty)

g. ___ ___anket (covering for a bed)

h. ___ ___anner (tool)

Consonant Clusters

Name _____

1. **Write each word below the correct picture.**

nest	fist	ant	hump
stump	hand	raft	desk

a. _____ b. _____ c. _____ d. _____

e. _____ f. _____ g. _____ h. _____

2. **Ring all the words that end in nt. Then write them on the lines below.**

b	e	n	t	p	b	s
s	t	h	w	l	l	p
e	e	u	e	a	u	e
n	n	n	n	n	n	n
t	t	t	t	t	t	t

_____ _____

_____ _____

_____ _____

_____ _____

3. **Choose the correct word for each sentence.**

grunt	mask	desk	plant
pond	fist	trunk	mend

a. An elephant has a _____.

b. He hit him with his _____.

c. The seed grew into a _____.

d. I sit at a _____ in my classroom.

e. I wore a _____ over my face.

f. A pig can _____.

g. I will _____ the broken toy.

h. We caught the fish in the _____.

Consonant Clusters

Name _____

1. **Write each word below the correct picture.**

gift	stamp	bolt	mask
colt	post	clamp	tent

a. _____ b. _____ c. _____ d. _____

e. _____ f. _____ g. _____ h. _____

2. Each word can be linked to a word below. The first one has been done for you.

stamp	nest	wash	west
crust	damp	wept	stump

a. letter   **stamp**   e. dry _____

b. bird _____   f. water _____

c. tree _____   g. cried _____

d. bread _____   h. east _____

3. **Use a word to complete each sentence.**

last	lamp	slept	belt
tuft	wind	cost	melt

a. The hot sun made the chocolate _____.

b. The tired baby _____ in the cot.

c. The _____ showed us the way in the darkness.

d. The strong _____ blew over the trees.

e. Ravi came first and Billy came _____ in the race.

f. The goat ate a _____ of grass.

g. The _____ of the toy is five pounds.

h. I wore a _____ around my waist.

Consonant Clusters

Name _____

1. **Write in pairs the words that contain the same sound unit.**

light	four	hose	might
mouth	south	pour	close

_____   _____   _____   _____

_____   _____   _____   _____

2. **Use an ng word to complete each sentence.**

wring	hungry	young	sprang
finger	angry	wrong	string

a. We tied the _____ around the parcel.

b. The boy bent his _____ playing basketball.

c. The leopard _____ onto the back of the antelope.

d. As I had not eaten all morning I was very _____.

e. The cow is old but its calf is _____.

f. I had to _____ out my towel when it fell in the river.

g. I was _____ because he had lost all my pencils.

h. This sum is right but this one is _____.

3. **Find the eight 'igh = long i sound' words in the grid. Then write them on the lines.**

n	i	g	h	t	h	m
l	i	g	h	t	i	i
s	i	g	h	t	g	g
t	i	g	h	t	h	h
f	r	i	g	h	t	t
b	r	i	g	h	t	x

_____   _____

_____   _____

_____   _____

_____   _____

Answers to Consonant Clusters

Answers to page 22

snail, cloud, skate, shout, stole

Answers to page 23

1 bread, cricket, bridle, cradle, flower, plate

2 stir, stamp, stream, stairs, storm, sting, straw, stove

3 **red:** trunk, tractor, trail, track, trick, treat, triangle, train, tramp

blue: sponge, spark, spent, speak, spine, spoil, spring, spray

green: scrap, scar, scarf, school, scooter, scout, score, scrub,

Answers to page 24

1 **red:** crocodile, swan, snail, sparrow, snake, spider

blue: shore, truck, plate, stain, spade, bread

2 **blue:** plum, gravy, bread, fruit, scone, spinach

red: scarf, skirt, slipper, trousers, glove, glasses

3 spear, sport, spade, spring, sparrow, spine

Answers to page 25

1 plug, triangle, swim, screw, sledge, skipping

2 truck, glow, planet, greet, slipper, scout

3 twig, twelve, twin, twitch, twice, twenty

Answers to page 26

1 crawl, cross, cradle, crocodile, crown, crane, cricket, crust

2 stump, straight, steak, stitch, stone, string, stable, story

3 green, grin; freckle, fresh; pretty, prince; smile, smack

Answers to page 27

1 snail, grape, spider, cloud, spear, plum, bridge, crowd

2 bread, cliff, flower, crown, plum, glove, smile, scone, snake, spire, triangle, swan

3 tractor, sparrow, grapes, planet, branch, flute

Answers to page 28

1 flood, flame, flock, flute, flea, fleet, flour, floor

2 blind, bridle, priest, brain, blood, prison, blanket, branch

3 sleep, snake, spider, glass, grain, plum

Answers to page 29

1 slave, sledge; snare, sneeze; cliff, climb; scar, scrap

2 sledge, spire, skate, cliff, steak, swallow

3 wasp, west, tales, pans, lips, cars, ports, logs

Answers to page 30

1 twice, twelve; smoke, smooth; slay, slip; straw, stump; trawl, track; flea, fly

2 broad, bridge, breakfast, bread, branch, bridle

3 crocodile, flea, plum, present, grin, clean, blanket, spanner

Answers to page 31

1 hump, ant, hand, desk, fist, nest, stump, raft

2 bent, sent, tent, hunt, went, plant, blunt, spent

3 trunk, fist, plant, desk, mask, grunt, mend, pond

Answers to page 32

1 bolt, tent, stamp, mask, gift, clamp, colt, post

2 nest, stump, crust, damp, wash, wept, west

3 melt, slept, lamp, wind, last, tuft, cost, belt

Answers to page 33

1 light, might;
four, pour;
hose, close;
mouth, south

2 string, finger, sprang, hungry, young, wring, angry, wrong

3 night, light, sight, tight, fright, bright, high, might (right is also correct)

Introduction to Identifying Phonemes

This is again a revision section, offering practice of the vowel phonemes taught at Key Stage 1, and specified in the National Literacy Strategy List 3.

As noted in Spelling Years 1–2, the rule for 'magic e' (a-e, i-e, o-e, u-e) is assumed to belong alongside long vowel phonemes, even though it is not listed explicitly in the National Literacy Strategy.

Spelling patterns should always be checked against sound patterns; e.g. make sure that children notice that some oo spellings have a long oo sound and some have a short oo sound, and that spellings like -ear may have several different pronunciations.

Identifying Phonemes

Name _____

1. **Write each word beside its meaning.**

   oo words

good	book	door	food
foot	room	roof	pool

   a. a place to swim _____

   b. it opens and shuts _____

   c. part of your leg _____

   d. we eat it _____

   e. it covers a house _____

   f. something we read _____

   g. not bad _____

   h. part of a house _____

2. **These words contain *ee*. Write each in the correct sentence.**

been	sleep	green
sheep	teeth	street

   a. We get wool from a _____ .

   b. Have you ever _____ to London?

   c. I clean my _____ after meals.

   d. I go to _____ at nine o'clock.

   e. We painted our house _____ .

   f. Our _____ has lots of houses.

3. **Add the missing letters to each word.**

   a. h__ __se   **b.** c__ __t   **c.** wind__ __

Identifying Phonemes

Name _____

1. Say each word then write each word under its picture.

   ar words

artist	shark	carpet	sharp
chart	army	party	cardigan

   a. _____ b. _____ c. _____ d. _____

   e. _____ f. _____ g. _____ h. _____

2. Add **ea** or **ai** to complete each word.

   a. tr___ ___n b. wh___ ___t c. str___ ___n d. b___ ___n

   e. d___ ___sy f. b___ ___ds g. ch___ ___n h. l___ ___f

3. How many four letter **i + e** words can you find? Write them on the lines.

s	i	z	e	h	i	v	e
w	i	s	e	v	i	n	e
r	i	p	e	b	i	k	e
l	i	f	e	w	i	p	e

   _____   _____

   _____   _____

   _____   _____

   _____

Identifying Phonemes

Name _____

1. **Each of these words contains i + e. Use each word to complete a sentence.**

ripe	invite	wipe	knife
hive	write	ninety	bike

   a. I rode my new _____ to school.

   b. Sally decided to _____ Ling to her party.

   c. We cut the meat with a sharp _____.

   d. The teacher asked us to _____ a story about snakes.

   e. The apples are now _____ and ready to eat.

   f. The farmer took the honey from the bees' _____.

   g. The number after eighty-nine is _____.

   h. On wet days you must _____ your feet before entering.

2. **Write each a + e word below the correct picture.**

blade	blaze	drake	grape
skate	whale	table	shave

   a. _____ b. _____ c. _____ d. _____

   e. _____ f. _____ g. _____ h. _____

3. **Add i + e or a + e to complete each word.**

   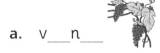

   a. v__n__ b. b__k__ c. n__n__ [9]

   d. m__n__ e. lemon__d__ f. l__n__

Identifying Phonemes

Name _____

1. Each word in the box contains an **ea** or **ear** sound. Write each under its picture.

peach	steam	spear	leap
tear	ear	bean	leaf

a. _____ b. _____ c. _____ d. _____

e. _____ f. _____ g. _____ h. _____

2. Add **ar** = long **ar** sound or **ai** = long **a** sound to complete each word.

a. sh__ __k   b. tr__ __n   c. d__ __sy   d. ch__ __n

e. f__ __m   f. c__ __pet   g. p__ __ty   h. dr__ __n

3. Each word in the box contains **ck**. Write the word below the correct picture.

bucket	chicken	flock	stick
clock	cricket	lock	brick

a. _____ b. _____ c. _____ d. _____

e. _____ f. _____ g. _____ h. _____

39

Identifying Phonemes

Name _____

1. **Each word in the box contains o + e. Use each to complete a sentence.**

hoe	toe	stole	stove
open	chose	joke	broken

   a. The thief _____ the precious diamonds.

   b. Mike _____ the larger of the two cakes.

   c. One door is shut but the other is _____.

   d. The gardener used a _____ to pull out the weeds.

   e. I put the pot of water on the _____ to heat it.

   f. We played a funny _____ on our teacher.

   g. When it dropped onto the floor the glass was _____.

   h. Dave hurt his big _____ when he kicked the ball.

2. **Find or words in the grid. Write them in the spaces. There are over ten or words.**

t	h	o	r	n	b	f
s	c	o	r	e	e	o
s	t	o	r	y	f	r
s	p	o	r	t	o	g
n	o	r	t	h	r	e
f	o	r	t	y	e	t
s	w	o	r	d	x	x
s	x	i	l	o	r	d

   _____   _____

   _____   _____

   _____   _____

   _____   _____

   _____   _____

3. **These words have been cramped together. Find and write each beside its picture.**

maskcalfbasketglassbathgrass

   a. _____   **b.** _____   **c.** _____

   d. _____   **e.** _____   **f.** _____

Identifying Phonemes

Name _____

1. **Each word contains an *ea* or *ear* sound. Use each in a sentence.**

peach	tears	cream	teacher	year
steam	dream	wheat	leak	leaves

   a. The rusty pipe began to _____.

   b. Last night I had a _____ about snakes.

   c. I ate a juicy _____ at lunch time.

   d. The _____ from the boiling water burnt his hand.

   e. There are twelve months in one _____.

   f. We raked up the autumn _____ on the path.

   g. The farmer sowed a field of _____.

   h. My _____ told me a story about elephants.

   i. The unhappy girl had _____ streaming down her cheeks.

   j. I like to eat scones with jam and _____.

2. **Each word contains an *ee* or *eer* sound. Match each to its meaning.**

knee	sheet	beef	deer	freeze
sheep	weed	cheese	thirteen	peep

   a. a food made from milk _____

   b. a joint of the leg _____

   c. an unwanted plant _____

   d. the meat of cattle _____

   e. to take a quick look _____

   f. a number _____

   g. an animal with antlers _____

   h. it is found on a bed _____

   i. animals that give us wool _____

   j. to turn water into a solid _____

3. **Find ten *ee* or *ea* words in the grid. Write them here.**

w	s	p	e	e	p	d	d	w	c
h	h	d	e	l	e	t	r	e	r
e	e	e	y	e	a	r	e	e	e
a	e	e	k	a	c	g	a	d	a
t	t	r	k	k	h	m	m	k	m

_____ _____

_____ _____

_____ _____

_____ _____

_____ _____

Identifying Phonemes

Name _____

1. Circle the two words in each line that contain the same sound.

   a. wash thorn steel worn   **e.** load hike trike mane

   b. relay thick blew stew   **f.** gaze blaze chose hare

   c. year croak fear circle   **g.** drake stove drove gaze

   d. spark loose noise shark   **h.** drain strain join year

2. Each word can be linked to a word below. Write each **er** word beside its link word.

   er words

spider	finger	thunder	shiver
timber	rubber	tiger	driver

   a. lightning _____   **e.** cold _____

   b. web _____   **f.** hand _____

   c. wood _____   **g.** ball _____

   d. lion _____   **h.** car _____

3. Add **wh**, **sh** or **th** to complete each word.

   a. ___ ___isper (to talk quietly)   **f.** mou___ ___ (opening for food)

   b. ___ ___irsty (needing a drink of water)   **g.** poli___ ___ (to make shiny)

   c. ___ ___isker (found on a cat's face)   **h.** ___ ___ale (large ocean mammal)

   d. fini___ ___ (to end)   **i.** ___ ___istle (something you blow to make a sound)

   e. ___ ___adow (formed by the sun)   **j.** ___ ___rone (seat of a king or queen)

Identifying Phonemes

Name _____

1. **Say each word, then match each one to its meaning.**

    u + e words

flute	true	glue	huge
prune	perfume	picture	useless

    What does it mean?

    a. a dried plum _____

    b. the opposite of false

    _____

    c. very large _____

    d. having no use _____

    e. a sticky substance _____

    f. sweet smelling _____

    g. a musical instrument _____

    h. a painting or drawing

    _____

2. **Add ai or ea to complete each sentence.**

    a. In the city square there was a large fount___ ___n.

    b. It is n___ ___rly half-past three.

    c. I put some cr___ ___m on my strawberries.

    d. In summer the wh___ ___t is harvested.

    e. There is some yellow p___ ___nt in the pot.

    f. There is a d___ ___sy growing in the garden.

    g. We saw st___ ___m coming off the boiling water.

    h. One ruler is crooked and one ruler is str___ ___ght.

3. **Can you spot six soft c words in the box? Write each below its picture.**

pencilmicecityricefencerace

    a. _____   **b.** _____   **c.** _____

    d. _____   **e.** _____   **f.** _____

Identifying Phonemes

Name _____

1. **Use each word to complete a sentence.**

   or words

torch	pork	storm	before
sword	thorn	sport	shore

   a. The knight used a sharp _____ to kill the dragon.

   b. The shipwrecked sailors swam towards the _____.

   c. We must leave here _____ it begins to rain.

   d. The lion has a _____ in its paw.

   e. A violent _____ shook the city last night.

   f. The meat of a pig is called _____.

   g. I used a powerful _____ to see my way in the dark.

   h. Football is a popular _____ in England.

2. **Add *ee* or *oo* to complete each word.**

   a. In the icebox the water began to fr___ ___ze.

   b. A beautiful butterfly hatched from the coc___ ___n.

   c. Some paper is rough while some of it is sm___ ___th.

   d. Sally tore the sl___ ___ve on her shirt.

   e. The princess began to kn___ ___l in front of the queen.

   f. The mice began to gnaw at the ch___ ___se.

   g. When the wheel lost its nuts it became l___ ___se.

   h. This mother hen has a large br___ ___d of chickens.

3. **Find seven words in the grid that contain *ck*. Then write them on the lines.**

c	r	i	c	k	e	t
b	u	c	k	e	t	b
p	a	c	k	e	t	l
t	h	i	c	k	x	a
b	l	o	c	k	z	c
t	r	i	c	k	x	k

   _____   _____

   _____   _____

   _____   _____

   _____

Identifying Phonemes

Name _____

1. **Write each word beside its meaning.**

   i + e words

divide	rifle	trike	outside
arrive	sunrise	hive	ninety

   a. a number _____

   b. opposite of depart _____

   c. a type of gun _____

   d. opposite of multiply _____

   e. opposite of inside _____

   f. opposite of sunset _____

   g. home for bees _____

   h. three-wheeled vehicle _____

2. **Find eight a + e words in the grid. Then write them on the lines.**

s	k	a	t	e	s	c
p	s	w	c	s	t	h
a	h	a	a	h	a	a
s	a	s	b	a	b	n
t	v	t	l	p	l	g
e	e	e	e	e	e	e

   _____ _____

   _____ _____

   _____ _____

   _____ _____

3. Each of these **o + e** words can be linked to a word below. The first one has been done for you.

   o + e words

toe	close	hoe	joke
open	woke	potatoes	stove

   a. foot ___**toe**___

   b. shut _____

   c. near _____

   d. slept _____

   e. rake _____

   f. chips _____

   g. cook _____

   h. funny _____

Answers to Identifying Phonemes

Answers to page 36

1 pool, door, foot, food, roof, book, good, room

2 sheep, been, teeth, sleep, green, street

3 horse, coat, window

Answers to page 37

1 army, shark, sharp, cardigan, artist, party, carpet, chart

2 train, wheat, strain, bean, daisy, beads, chain, leaf

3 size, hive, wise, vine, ripe, bike, life, wipe

Answers to page 38

1 bike, invite, knife, write, ripe, hive, ninety, wipe

2 whale, table, skate, drake, blade, blaze, grape, shave

3 vine, bike, nine, mane, lemonade, line

Answers to page 39

1 tear, spear, leaf, ear, peach, bean, steam, leap

2 shark, train, daisy, chain, farm, carpet, party, drain

3 chicken, cricket, stick, brick, clock, bucket, lock, flock

Answers to page 40

1 stole, chose, open, hoe, stove, joke, broken, toe

2 answers include: thorn, score, story, sport, north, forty, sword, lord, for, forge

3 bath, grass, mask, basket, glass, calf

Answers to page 41

1 leak, dream, peach, steam, year, leaves, wheat, teacher, tears, cream

2 cheese, knee, weed, beef, peep, thirteen, deer, sheet, sheep, freeze

3 peach, sheet, peep, deer, leak, dream, year, wheat, weed, cream

Answers to page 42

1 thorn, worn; blew, stew; year, fear; spark, shark; hike, trike; gaze, blaze; stove, drove; drain, strain

2 thunder, spider, timber, tiger, shiver, finger, rubber, driver

3 whisper, thirsty, whisker, finish, shadow, mouth, polish, whale, whistle, throne

Answers to page 43

1 prune, true, huge, useless, glue, perfume, flute, picture

2 fountain, nearly, cream, wheat, paint, daisy, steam, straight

3 city, mice, rice, pencil, race, fence

Answers to page 44

1 sword, shore, before, thorn, storm, pork, torch, sport

2 freeze, cocoon, smooth, sleeve, kneel, cheese, loose, brood

3 answers include: cricket, bucket, packet, thick, block, trick, black

Answers to page 45

1 ninety, arrive, rifle, divide, outside, sunrise, hive, trike

2 skate, paste, shave, waste, cable, shape, table or stable, change

3 open, close, woke, hoe, potatoes, stove, joke

Introduction and Answers to Compound Words

The National Literacy Strategy refers specifically to compound words at several points: Y2T2, Y3T2, and Y4T3; by Y4T3 the justification is: 'to recognise that they can aid spelling even where pronunciation obscures it, e.g. handbag, cupboard'.

Answers to page 48

1 grasshopper, windmill, crossroads, tugboat, jellyfish, ladybird, toothbrush, haystack

2 lighthouse, bulldog, necklace, spaceship, starfish, overcoat, waterfall, football

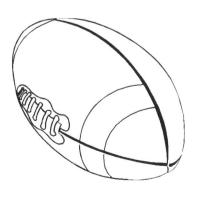

Answers to page 49

1 toothpaste, baseball, overcoat, windmill, postbox, campfire, waterfall, armchair

2 tugboat, airport, lighthouse, rooftop, necklace, pancake

3 strawberry, horseshoe, ladybird, sunlight, matchbox, anywhere, broomstick, playtime, footpath, tablecloth

Compound Words

Name _____

1. **Complete each compound word.**

    Use these words.

fish	bird	brush	stack
boat	roads	mill	hopper

    a. grass_____ **b.** wind_____ **c.** cross_____ **d.** tug_____

    e. jelly_____ **f.** lady_____ **g.** tooth_____ **h.** hay_____

2. **Complete each compound word.**

    Use these words.

ship	house	coat	dog
fish	lace	fall	ball

    a. light_____ **b.** bull_____ **c.** neck_____ **d.** space_____

    e. star_____ **f.** over_____ **g.** water_____ **h.** foot_____

Compound Words

Name _____

1. **Complete each compound word.**

   Use these words.

ball	mill	coat	paste
fire	chair	fall	box

   a. tooth_____   **b.** base_____   **c.** over_____   **d.** wind_____

   e. post_____   **f.** camp_____   **g.** water_____   **h.** arm_____

2. **Unjumble the letters in brackets to make compound words.**

   a. tug (obat) _____   **b.** air (ptor) _____   **c.** light (ohuse) _____

   d. roof (tpo) _____   **e.** neck (alce) _____   **f.** pan (kcea) _____

3. **Choose a word from List B to complete each compound word in List A.**

   List A

straw_____	any_____
horse_____	broom_____
lady_____	play_____
sun_____	foot_____
match_____	table_____

   List B

where	bird
time	light
cloth	shoe
berry	box
path	stick

Introduction and Answers to Plurals

In the National Literacy Strategy, the rules for making plural forms are treated more under Sentence level work and Grammatical awareness than under Spelling.

Three rules are included in this section:
- simple plurals, ending in s;
- words ending in x, ch, s, ss or sh, adding es;
- and words ending in y, where if the y is not preceded by a vowel the y changes to ies;
- and finally, irregular plural forms.

Answers to page 51

1 cats, horses, cows, chairs, disks, tables, hats, gloves

2 birds, chairs, plants, books, apples, seats, desks, cows

3 branches, matches, watches, peaches

Answers to page 52

1 boxes, foxes, bushes, churches

2 days, toys, boys, donkeys, keys, jockeys

3 men, teeth, geese, mice

Answers to page 53

1 tables, pencils, trees, slices, hats, seats, birds, horses

2 bunches, churches, catches, peaches, beaches, stitches

3 buses, wishes, dresses, glasses, foxes, boxes, gases, guesses

Answers to page 54

1 matches, batches, trenches, patches, punches, branches

2 keys, toys, turkeys, donkeys

3 flies, cries, poppies, cities, stories, ladies, berries

Plurals

Name _____

1. **Make each word mean more than one.**

   a. one **cat**   two _____

   b. one **horse** two _____

   c. one **cow**   three _____

   d. one **chair** two _____

   e. one **disk**   two _____

   f. one **table** three _____

   g. one **hat**   two _____

   h. one **glove** two _____

2. **Complete each sentence. Make the word in brackets mean more than one.**

   a. We counted ten _____ flying overhead. (**bird**)

   b. I put all the _____ back in the room. (**chair**)

   c. Lots of _____ were growing in the garden. (**plant**)

   d. I read three _____ last week. (**book**)

   e. There are six _____ left on the tree. (**apple**)

   f. We had to stack all the _____ in the gymnasium. (**seat**)

   g. All the _____ are in his office. (**desk**)

   h. Several _____ are in the meadow. (**cow**)

3. **Add *es* to make each word mean more than one.**

   a. one **branch** two _____   **b.** one **match** two _____

   c. one **watch** two _____   **d.** one **peach** two _____

Plurals

Name _____

1. **Make each word mean more than one.**

   a. one **box**   two _____

   b. one **fox**   three _____

   c. one **bush**   three _____

   d. one **church**   two _____

2. **Make the word in brackets mean more than one. Complete each sentence.**

   a. There are only ten _____ until Christmas. (**day**)

   b. My best friend has lots of _____. (**toy**)

   c. I saw three _____ steal the fruit. (**boy**)

   d. There are four _____ in the paddock. (**donkey**)

   e. I cannot find all the _____ to these locks. (**key**)

   f. The _____ are mounting their horses. (**jockey**)

3. **Make each word mean more than one.**

   a. one **man**   two _____

   b. one **tooth**   four _____

   c. one **goose**   three _____

   d. one **mouse**   two _____

Plurals

Name _____

1. **Complete each sentence. Make the word in brackets mean more than one.**

    a. We moved five _____ into the classroom. (table)

    b. Asha has three more _____ than I have. (pencil)

    c. Lots of big _____ grow in the park. (tree)

    d. Nick ate three _____ of bread for lunch. (slice)

    e. The boys' _____ are on the pegs. (hat)

    f. All the _____ in the playground are being painted. (seat)

    g. We saw several _____ flying over the lake. (bird)

    h. The jockeys urged their _____ to run faster. (horse)

2. **Add _es_ to the word in brackets. Complete each sentence.**

    a. I picked three _____ of flowers. (bunch)

    b. There are four _____ in our street. (church)

    c. Mary took three _____ during the match. (catch)

    d. Anna picked two _____ from the tree. (peach)

    e. There are lots of beautiful _____ around here. (beach)

    f. I had to sew ten _____ in the torn shirt. (stitch)

3. **Add _es_ to the word in brackets. Complete each sentence.**

    a. Lots of _____ bring children to our school. (bus)

    b. The genie gave the boy three _____. (wish)

    c. The girls left their old _____ on the bed. (dress)

    d. Some of the _____ were broken when the box fell. (glass)

    e. We saw three _____ in the field. (fox)

    f. Put the toys away in those cardboard _____. (box)

    g. Oxygen and nitrogen are two _____. (gas)

    h. I'll give you two _____ to see if you can get it right. (guess)

Plurals

Name _____

1. **Add es to make each word mean more than one.**

   a. There are seven _____ left in the box. (**match**)

   b. The baker cooked four _____ of bread. (**batch**)

   c. The roadworkers dug four _____. (**trench**)

   d. I have two _____ in my trousers. (**patch**)

   e. The boxer threw six _____ in the second round. (**punch**)

   f. The tree pruner cut down three _____. (**branch**)

2. **Make each word mean more than one.**

   a. one **key**   two _____

   b. one **toy**   three _____

   c. one **turkey**   two _____

   d. one **donkey**   two _____

3. **Make the word in brackets mean more than one.**
   The first one has been done for you.

   a. Lots of _____**flies**_____ landed on the cake. (**fly**)

   b. We could hear the sad _____ of the baby. (**cry**)

   c. I picked two _____ and put them in a vase. (**poppy**)

   d. There are many large _____ in Europe. (**city**)

   e. Our teacher read us two _____ about dinosaurs. (**story**)

   f. At least five _____ attended the meeting. (**lady**)

   g. We ate all the ripe _____ on the bush. (**berry**)

Introduction and Answers to Silent and Soft Letters

The National Literacy Strategy refers to silent letters in **Y2T2 W10**: 'to investigate, spell and read words with silent letters, e.g. knee, gnat, wrinkle'.

We also include soft c and soft g in this section, the rule being that both are sounded as soft letters when followed by e, i or y.

Answers to page 56

1 comb, palm, hour, knee, half, calf, knife

2
lamb, b;
wrap, w;
bomb, b;
climb, b;
gnat, g;
know, k;
scent, c;
write, w

3 crumb, thistle, scent, limb, wrong, plumber, lamb, yolk

Answers to page 57

1 city, pencil, fence, face, ice, race, mice, circus

2 tooth, cocoon, rooster, bathroom, school, bedroom, zoo, goose, school has a silent h

3
calf, half;
last, fast;
glass, grass;
after; mask

Answers to page 58

1 giant, giraffe, bridge, cabbage, page, orange, edge, cage

2 lose, words, hose, oil, peak, harm, ape, hoe

3 blaze, blade, pane, skate, grape

Silent and Soft Letters

Name _____

1. **Choose a word to complete each sentence.**

calf	hour	comb	half
knee	palm	knife	

   a. I used a _____ to tidy my hair.

   b. A large _____ tree grew in our garden.

   c. There are sixty minutes in one _____.

   d. When he fell over he hurt his _____.

   e. Two quarters make one _____.

   f. The cow and its _____ were placed in the yard.

   g. Effie cut the meat with the sharp _____.

2. **Circle the word with a silent letter in each group. Write the silent letter on the line.**

   a. paper   lamb   tablet   _____   e. gnat   soon   bold   _____

   b. wrap   silly   old   _____   f. step   know   box   _____

   c. window   grass   bomb   _____   g. scent   bottle   hand   _____

   d. nut   climb   little   _____   h. top   seven   write   _____

3. **Can you see where the silent letter in brackets should be added to each word? Write the word.**

   a. (b) crum   _____   e. (w) rong   _____
   small piece of bread   not right

   b. (t) thisle   _____   f. (b) plumer   _____
   prickly plant   a person who mends taps and pipes

   c. (c) sent   _____   g. (b) lam   _____
   perfume   young sheep

   d. (b) lim   _____   h. (l) yok   _____
   part of the body   part of an egg

Silent and Soft Letters

Name _____

1. **Say each word in the box. Then match each word to a picture.**

c becomes soft **c** when followed by *e*, *i* or *y*

ice	race	city	fence
pencil	circus	face	mice

a. _____ b. _____ c. _____ d. _____

e. _____ f. _____ g. _____ h. _____

2. **Match each oo word to a picture. Can you spot a word with a silent letter?**

goose	tooth	school	bathroom
zoo	bedroom	rooster	cocoon

a. _____ b. _____ c. _____ d. _____

e. _____ f. _____ g. _____ h. _____

3. **Write each word under its letter string.**

glass	last	calf	half	grass	after	mask	fast

a. alf   b. ast   c. ass   d. aft   e. ask

_____   _____   _____   _____   _____

_____   _____   _____

Silent and Soft Letters

Name _____

1. Say each word in the box, then write each word beside its meaning.

g sounds like **j** when followed by e, i or y

cage	page	cabbage	giraffe
giant	orange	edge	bridge

a. a very, very large person _____

b. an animal with a long neck

_____

c. a span over a river _____

d. a leafy green vegetable _____

e. a part of a book _____

f. a colour or fruit _____

g. the side of something _____

h. where pet birds are kept

_____

2. **Drop the first letter to make a word that matches the definition.**

a. close – mislay something _____

b. swords – they are made of letters

_____

c. whose – it transports water _____

d. boil – we use it in cars _____

e. speak – top of a mountain

_____

f. charm – to hurt _____

g. cape – large animal _____

h. shoe – garden tool _____

3. Can you see that each **a + e** word in the box can be linked with a word below? Write each word beside its link word. The first one has been done for you.

blade	table	blaze
pane	grape	skate

a. chair **table**

b. fire _____

c. knife _____

d. glass _____

e. ice _____

f. vine _____

Introduction and Answers to Synonyms and Antonyms

Synonyms and antonyms are introduced in the National Literacy Strategy in Year 3 Term 1:

Y3T1 W17: to generate synonyms for high frequency words, e.g. big, little, like, good, nice, nasty;

Y3T1 W11: to use their knowledge of prefixes to generate new words from root words, especially antonyms.

This should lead children to start using thesauruses, as a further way of extending their vocabulary.

Answers to page 60

1 ring, boat, dish, baby, tale, little, wet, fall

2 down, stop, buy, winter, sit, alive, day, west

3 sad, closed, cold, dry, noisy

Answers to page 61

1 tiny, hate, smile, quick, story, rich, dress, stone

2 south, hard, high, asleep, slow, weak, happy, quiet

3 saw, our, now, key, two, win, who, rug, ate, dug

Answers to page 62

1 now, thin, dead, sick, tame, black, slow, close

2 huge, love, small, pale, narrow, close, yell, present

3 park, bank, mouse, four, funny, school, about

Answers to page 63

1 rich, together, many, hate, nothing, low, took, begin

2 unable, unlikely, unblock, uncurl, unbroken

3 disappear, discolour, dishonest, dislike, disused, disobey

Synonyms and Antonyms

Name _____

1. *Synonyms*. Write words together that have the same meaning.

little	baby	fall	ring
boat	tale	wet	dish

a. circle _____

b. ship _____

c. bowl _____

d. child _____

e. story _____

f. small _____

g. damp _____

h. drop _____

2. *Antonyms*. Match each word to its opposite.

sit	west	stop	day
buy	alive	down	winter

a. up _____

b. go _____

c. sell _____

d. summer _____

e. stand _____

f. dead _____

g. night _____

h. east _____

3. *Antonyms*. Read the first word in each line, then draw a ring around its opposite.

a. **happy** hurry sad cup

b. **open** chair door closed

c. **hot** hand smile cold

d. **wet** wind hard dry

e. **quiet** queen cake noisy

Synonyms and Antonyms

Name _____

1. *Synonyms*. Write words together that have the same meaning.

hate	rich	quick	stone
tiny	story	smile	dress

a. small _____

b. dislike _____

c. grin _____

d. fast _____

e. tale _____

f. wealthy _____

g. frock _____

h. rock _____

2. *Antonyms*. Read each word in the box, then write it next to its opposite below.

weak	south	high	asleep
hard	slow	quiet	happy

a. north _____

b. soft _____

c. low _____

d. awake _____

e. fast _____

f. strong _____

g. sad _____

h. loud _____

3. How many <u>three</u>-letter words can you find?

s	a	w	o	u	r
r	a	d	n	o	w
u	t	u	k	e	y
g	e	g	t	w	o
w	i	n	w	h	o

_____ _____ _____

_____ _____

_____ _____

_____

Synonyms and Antonyms

Name _____

1. *Antonyms.* Write each word beside its opposite.

tame	dead	close	now
sick	black	thin	slow

a. later _____

b. fat _____

c. alive _____

d. well _____

e. wild _____

f. white _____

g. fast _____

h. far _____

2. *Synonyms.* Read the first word, then circle the synonym.

a. (big) slow high (huge)

b. like car love lorry

c. little small house hill

d. light log hammer pale

e. thin book narrow bird

f. near bark close fast

g. shout tree leaf yell

h. gift laugh present blue

3. Write each word in the correct pattern.

mouse	school	funny	four
bank	about	park	

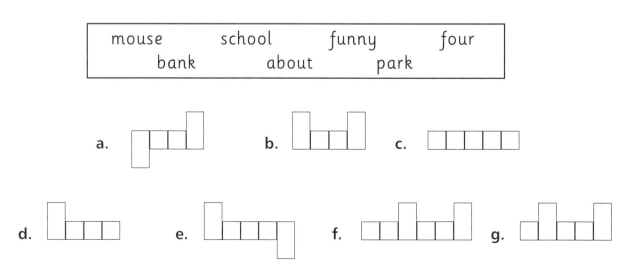

Synonyms and Antonyms

Name _____

1. *Antonyms*. Write each word beside its opposite.

low	begin	rich	took
many	hate	nothing	together

a. poor _____

b. apart _____

c. few _____

d. like _____

e. everything _____

f. high _____

g. gave _____

h. end _____

2. Make each word mean the opposite by adding the prefix un–.
Write the new words. The first one has been done for you.

a. happy **unhappy**

b. able _____

c. likely _____

d. block _____

e. curl _____

f. broken _____

3. Make each word mean the opposite by adding the prefix dis–.
Write the new words.

a. appear _____

b. colour _____

c. honest _____

d. like _____

e. used _____

f. obey _____

From Time-Savers for Teachers: Spelling Years 3-4. This page may be reproduced for classroom use.

63

Introduction to Suffixes

The National Literacy Strategy stresses the importance of understanding the form of the root word before adding suffixes -ly, -ed, or -ing:

Y3T1 W8: how the spellings of verbs alter when -ing is added;

Y3T2 W13: to recognise and spell common suffixes and how these influence word meanings, e.g. -ly, -ful, -less;

Y4T1 W7: to spell regular verb endings s, ed, ing (link to grammar work on tenses).

The stages involved are therefore separating the root word; applying a spelling rule to the word ending; and understanding how this changes the word class or the verb tense.

Suffixes

Name _____

1. **Add ly to each word. This changes them from adjectives to adverbs.**

    e.g.   friend + ly = **friendly**

    a. slow   _____   d. loud   _____

    b. quick   _____   e. nice   _____

    c. bright   _____   f. brave   _____

2. **Add y to each word. This changes them from nouns to adjectives.**

    a. wind + y = _____   e. snow + y = _____

    b. hill + y = _____   f. stink + y = _____

    c. rain + y = _____   g. smell + y = _____

    d. swamp + y = _____   h. storm + y = _____

3. **Write the root form of each verb. The first one has been done for you.**

    a. walking comes from **walk**   e. looking comes from _____

    b. hunting comes from _____   f. playing comes from _____

    c. showing comes from _____   g. running comes from _____

    d. fighting comes from _____   h. dashing comes from _____

From Time-Savers for Teachers: Spelling Years 3-4. This page may be reproduced for classroom use.

65

Suffixes

Name _____

1. Write the root form of each word.

   e.g. riding   comes from **ride**_____

   a. racing   comes from _____   e. baking   comes from _____

   b. hiking   comes from _____   f. hoping   comes from _____

   c. liking   comes from _____   g. coming   comes from _____

   d. making   comes from _____   h. taming   comes from _____

2. Add **ed** and **ing** to each word. The first one has been done for you.

		+ ed	+ ing
a.	rock	**rocked**	**rocking**
b.	jump	_____	_____
c.	splash	_____	_____
d.	bark	_____	_____
e.	clean	_____	_____
f.	cover	_____	_____
g.	walk	_____	_____

3. The suffix–less can be added to each of these words. Write the new words.
   The first one has been done for you.

   a. hope   **hopeless**_____   d. thought _____

   b. care   _____   e. speech _____

   c. hair   _____   f. count _____

Suffixes

Name _____

> **RULE:** When we add ed or ing to a word that ends in a short vowel and one consonant, double the consonant.
>
> e.g.   drop – dropped – dropping

1. **Add ed to the word in brackets and complete each sentence.**

   a. The girl _____ across the yard. (hop)

   b. Leanne _____ the wood with an axe. (chop)

   c. The car _____ at the corner. (stop)

   d. The leopard _____ the zebra to its den. (drag)

   e. Asha _____ her leg where she was hit by the ball. (rub)

2. **Now add ed to each of these words. Complete each sentence.**

   a. We _____ football yesterday. (play)

   b. I _____ the jet roar into the air. (watch)

   c. The frightened children _____ into the room. (rush)

   d. We _____ everywhere for the lost pencils. (look)

   e. The rocket _____ on the faraway planet. (land)

   f. Sally _____ me her new bicycle. (show)

3. **Add ing to the word in brackets. Don't forget to double the last letter. Complete each sentence.**

   a. Mike is _____ across the pool. (swim)

   b. The boys are _____ their excursion. (plan)

   c. I am going _____ with my father. (shop)

   d. The bees are _____ loudly. (hum)

   e. Ravi is _____ across the field. (run)

   f. We are _____ the rope into pieces. (cut)

Suffixes

Name _____

1. **Add ing to the word in brackets and complete each sentence.**

    a. The boys are _____ in the yard. (**play**)

    b. The ship is _____ beneath the water. (**sink**)

    c. I am _____ a glass of lemonade. (**drink**)

    d. Ling is _____ the other children her new bike. (**show**)

    e. I am _____ for a lost puppy. (**look**)

    f. Tom is _____ a meat pie for lunch. (**eat**)

    > **RULE:** When we add **ing** to words ending in silent **e** we drop the **e**.
    > e.g.   ice – icing

2. **Add ing to the word in brackets. Complete each sentence.**

    a. The cat is _____ the mouse. (**chase**)

    b. The boys are _____ to their friends. (**wave**)

    c. The chef is _____ some pies. (**bake**)

    d. The dog is _____ the stranger. (**bite**)

    e. The motorist is _____ the tyre on the car. (**change**)

3. **Write what each person is doing. Use the words in the box.**

brushing	sweeping	tasting
climbing	cooking	washing

    a. Katy is _____ the tree.   **d.** Joanne is _____ a meal.

    b. Raj is _____ his hair.   **e.** Leanne is _____ the food.

    c. Peter is _____ the path.   **f.** Tan is _____ up.

Suffixes

Name _____

1. **Add ed to the word in brackets. The first one has been done for you.**

   a. Yesterday Oona **played** cricket. (play)

   b. This morning I _____ my father wash the car. (help)

   c. I _____ at the silly boy. (shout)

   d. The dog _____ at the stranger. (growl)

   e. I _____ some steak for my tea. (cook)

   f. Yesterday Ling _____ a tree. (plant)

   g. I dried the dishes and Peter _____ them. (wash)

   h. The tall mountains _____ their way. (block)

2. **Write the base word from which each word came.**

   e.g. barked comes from **bark**

   a. lifted   comes from _____   e. bathed   comes from _____

   b. covered   comes from _____   f. asked   comes from _____

   c. tricked   comes from _____   g. picked   comes from _____

   d. rowed   comes from _____   h. pulled   comes from _____

3. **Add e to the end of each word.**

   e.g.   can   **cane**

   a. tap   _____   e. bit   _____

   b. pin   _____   f. pan   _____

   c. cap   _____   g. rid   _____

   d. not   _____   h. win   _____

Suffixes

Name _____

1. **Add ing to each word. Complete each sentence.**

    a. Sanjit is _____ her dress. (**wash**)

    b. Joanne is _____ the football. (**kick**)

    c. Tom is _____ his kite. (**fly**)

    d. Raj is _____ the teacher. (**help**)

    e. The boy is _____ out of the tree. (**fall**)

    f. Tan is _____ the water. (**drink**)

    g. My mum is _____ the car out of the driveway. (**back**)

    h. Chan is _____ the yellow flowers. (**smell**)

2. **Write the base word from which each word is made. The first one has been done for you.**

    e.g. shopping   comes from   **shop**

    a. hopping   comes from _____   **e.** running   comes from _____

    b. skipping   comes from _____   **f.** swimming comes from _____

    c. chopping comes from _____   **g.** putting   comes from _____

    d. mopping   comes from _____   **h.** stepping   comes from _____

3. **Write the base word from which each word is made. The first one has been done for you.**

    e.g. stealing   comes from   **steal**

    a. filling   comes from _____   **e.** helping   comes from _____

    b. feeling   comes from _____   **f.** playing   comes from _____

    c. weeping   comes from _____   **g.** picking   comes from _____

    d. climbing   comes from _____   **h.** weeding   comes from _____

Suffixes

Name _____

1. **Make the word in brackets end in ed.**

    a. I dried the dishes after Tom _____ them. (wash)

    b. I _____ the rocket soar into the air. (watch)

    c. Rebecca _____ the ball across the yard. (kick)

    d. We _____ papers into the bin. (stuff)

    e. Shaheen _____ some muffins on the fire. (toast)

    f. Tan _____ the glass off the shelf. (knock)

2. **Add ed to the word in brackets. Don't forget to double the last letter.**

    a. Chan _____ up the spilt water. (mop)

    b. Tom _____ the tables clean. (scrub)

    c. Ling _____ her new pony on the neck. (pat)

    d. The horse _____ across the paddock. (trot)

    e. The leopard _____ its prey to its den. (drag)

    f. The children _____ onto the escalator. (step)

3. **Add ing and ed to each word. Remember you may have to double some letters.**

	+ ing	+ ed			+ ing	+ ed
e.g. hop	**hopping**	**hopped**				
a. plan	_____	_____		e. rush	_____	_____
b. wish	_____	_____		f. last	_____	_____
c. trip	_____	_____		g. paint	_____	_____
d. clean	_____	_____		h. clap	_____	_____

Suffixes

Name _____

1. **Write the base word. The first one has been done for you.**

   e.g. riding   comes from   **ride**

   a. skating   comes from _____   **e.** racing   comes from _____

   b. hiking   comes from _____   **f.** facing   comes from _____

   c. liking   comes from _____   **g.** striking   comes from _____

   d. taming   comes from _____   **h.** moving   comes from _____

2. **Write an action word in each sentence. Use a word from the box.**
   The first one has been done for you.

swim	hit	sit
dig	chop	scrub

   a. Jacob is **swimming**.

   b. Shaheen is _____ in the chair.

   c. Ravi is _____ Ben.

   d. David is _____ some wood.

   e. Tom is _____ the floor.

   f. Sam is _____ up the garden.

3. **Add ly to each word in brackets. Complete each sentence.**

   e.g. Henry is accepting the award **proudly**. (proud)

   a. Cath did her work _____. (bad)

   b. We walked _____ along the road. (slow)

   c. The children sang the song _____. (loud)

   d. The sun was shining _____. (bright)

   e. The athletes ran _____ across the field. (quick)

   f. The small boy faced the bully _____. (brave)

Suffixes

Name _____

> **RULE:** Silent e goes away when ing comes to stay.

1. Add ing to each word in brackets. Make sure you drop the final e.

   a. Tim is __**riding**__ his bicycle. (ride)

   b. Asha is _____ a toy car. (make)

   c. Joe is _____ his money for Christmas presents. (save)

   d. The cows are _____ along the road. (come)

   e. Mrs Wong is _____ her dog to the vet. (take)

   f. Callan is _____ in the bushes. (hide)

   g. I am _____ a chocolate cake. (bake)

   h. Bianca is _____ a story about snakes. (write)

2. Add ing to the word in brackets. Make sure you double the final consonant.

   a. Jana is __**sitting**__ on a chair. (sit)

   b. The car is _____ at the corner. (stop)

   c. Raj is _____ up the spilt milk. (mop)

   d. My mother is _____ some wood. (chop)

   e. We are _____ across the puddle. (step)

   f. Are you _____ enough to eat? (get)

   g. Our team is _____ the match. (win)

   h. Tom is _____ across the schoolyard. (run)

3. Add ing to each word. Remember to refer to the rules you know.

a. fly _____	**b.** scrub _____	**c.** like _____
d. shop _____	**e.** stick _____	**f.** take _____
g. pat _____	**h.** trot _____	**i.** shine _____
j. hit _____	**k.** drag _____	**l.** try _____
m. ring _____	**n.** come _____	**o.** pace _____

Answers to Suffixes

Answers to page 65

1 slowly, quickly, brightly, loudly, nicely, bravely

2 windy, hilly, rainy, swampy, snowy, stinky, smelly, stormy

3 walk, hunt, show, fight, look, play, run, dash

Answers to page 66

1 race, hike, like, make, bake, hope, come, tame

2 jumped, jumping; splashed, splashing; barked, barking; cleaned, cleaning; covered, covering; walked, walking

3 careless, hairless, thoughtless, speechless, countless

Answers to page 67

1 hopped, chopped, stopped, dragged, rubbed

2 played, watched, rushed, looked, landed, showed

3 swimming, planning, shopping, humming, running, cutting

Answers to page 68

1 playing, sinking, drinking, showing, looking, eating

2 chasing, waving, baking, biting, changing

3 climbing, brushing, sweeping, cooking, tasting, washing

Answers to page 69

1 helped, shouted, growled, cooked, planted, washed, blocked

2 lift, cover, trick, row, bath, ask, pick, pull

3 tape, pine, cape, note, bite, pane, ride, wine

Answers to page 70

1 washing, kicking, flying, helping, falling, drinking, backing, smelling

2 hop, skip, chop, mop, run, swim, put, step

3 fill, feel, weep, climb, help, play, pick, weed

Answers to page 71

1 washed, watched, kicked, stuffed, toasted, knocked

2 mopped, scrubbed, patted, trotted, dragged, stepped

3 planning, planned; wishing, wished; tripping, tripped; cleaning, cleaned; rushing, rushed; lasting, lasted; painting, painted; clapping, clapped

Answers to page 72

1 skate, hike, like, tame, race, face, strike, move

2 sitting, hitting, chopping, scrubbing, digging

3 badly, slowly, loudly, brightly, quickly, bravely

Answers to page 73

1 making, saving, coming, taking, hiding, baking, writing

2 stopping, mopping, chopping, stepping, getting, winning, running

3 flying, scrubbing, liking, shopping, sticking, taking, patting, trotting, shining, hitting, dragging, trying, ringing, coming, pacing

Introduction and Answers to Double Consonants

Whereas double consonants at the end of words are introduced in Year 1 Term 2 (ff, ll, ss), double consonants in the middle of two-syllable words come much later:

Y4T1 W6: to spell two-syllable words containing double consonants, e.g. bubble, kettle, common.

It is worth demonstrating that double consonants usually follow short vowel sounds, whereas single consonants indicate long vowel sounds: e.g. gabble and gable, riffle and rifle.

Answers to page 76

hammer, balloon, button, bottle, lollipop, carrot, fiddle, squirrel, arrow, glass, kettle, parrot, slipper, middle, collar, rabbit, kitten, kennel

Answers to page 77

1 bottle, burrow, puppet, parrot, paddle, lolly, flippers, mess

2 pillow, skull, arrow, kettle, lollipop, pretty, hammer, button

3 puddle, swallow, apple, blossom, slipper, saddle, squirrel, follow, dress, happy

Double Consonants

Name _____

Add double letters to complete each word.

a. ha___ ___er

b. ba___ ___oon

c. bu___ ___on

d. bo___ ___le

e. lo___ ___ipop

f. ca___ ___ot

g. fi___ ___le

h. squi___ ___el

i. a___ ___ow

j. gla___ ___

k. ke___ ___le

l. pa___ ___ot

m. sli___ ___er

n. mi___ ___le

o. co___ ___ar

p. ra___ ___it

q. ki___ ___en

r. ke___ ___el

Double Consonants

Name _____

1. **Circle the correct word in brackets.**

   a. I filled the (battle **bottle**) with water.

   b. A wild rabbit digs a (barrow burrow).

   c. A wooden doll is called a (poppet puppet).

   d. A (carrot parrot) is a type of bird.

   e. I used a (paddle puddle) to row the boat.

   f. I ate a chocolate (lolly holly).

   g. A dolphin has (flippers flappers).

   h. The storm left a terrible (mess mass) in the street.

2. **Match each word in the box to a clue below.**

pretty	pillow	skull	kettle
lollipop	hammer	arrow	button

   a. it's found on a bed _____

   b. the bony part of your head _____

   c. a bow and _____

   d. you boil water in it _____

   e. it is sweet to suck _____

   f. nice to look at _____

   g. it bangs in nails _____

   h. it is found on a shirt _____

3. **Add ss, dd, pp, rr, or ll to make words that fit the meanings.**

   a. pu___ ___le (a pool of water)

   b. swa___ ___ow (a small bird)

   c. a___ ___le (a fruit)

   d. blo___ ___om (flowers on a tree)

   e. sli___ ___er (footwear)

   f. sa___ ___le (seat on a horse)

   g. squi___ ___el (a furry animal)

   h. fo___ ___ow (to go after)

   i. dre___ ___ (a type of clothing)

   j. ha___ ___y (opposite of sad)

Introduction to Homophones

Homophones are inevitably a source of confusion, because the different words sound the same but are spelt in different ways according to meaning and origins, thus proving how difficult the English language is to learn, in not having regular sound/spelling correspondence.

Many teachers therefore prefer to keep homophones apart until they start causing difficulty; but the National Literacy Strategy suggests they should be explicitly taught:

Y4T1 W6: to distinguish between the spelling and meanings of common homophones, e.g. to/two/too; they're/their/there; piece/peace.

Often the only strategy, if you're not sure which spelling is right and cannot trace the word origin, is to check in the dictionary and then try to memorise the answer.

It is interesting that homonyms are introduced earlier, presumably because they cause less confusion in spelling:

Y3T3 W14: to explore homonyms which have the same spelling but multiple meanings and explain how the meanings can be distinguished in context, e.g. form (shape or document), wave (gesture, shape or motion).

Homophones

Name _____

Choose the correct word for each picture. Write it on the lines.

a. sun   son

_____

b. tow   toe

_____

c. two   too

_____

d. see   sea

_____

e. ate   eight

_____

f. hair   hare

_____

g. rose   rows

_____

h. pair   pear

_____

i. sail   sale

_____

j. tale   tail

_____

k. mail   male

_____

l. knot   not

_____

m. flour   flower

_____

n. dear   deer

_____

o. rain   rein

_____

p. some   sum

4 + 6 = 10

_____

q. pear   pair

_____

r. been   bean

_____

s. plain   plane

_____

t. would   wood

_____

Homophones

Name _____

1. **Write the word that matches the picture.**

   a. sun   son

   _____

   b. tow   toe

   _____

   c. two   too

   _____

   d. ate   eight

   _____

   e. sail   sale

   _____

   f. hair   hare

   _____

2. **Choose the correct word to complete each sentence.**

   a. We should arrive in about an (our   hour).

   b. The cat licked its (fur   fir).

   c. We watched the ships sailing on the (sea   see).

   d. Our teacher told us a (tail   tale) about a dinosaur.

   e. When the fire started we decided to (flea   flee) quickly.

3. **In the grid find a homophone for each word. Write them on the lines.**

s	e	e	o	n	e	h
s	t	a	t	e	x	a
u	w	t	o	e	x	r
n	o	t	a	i	l	e

knot _____   too _____

sea _____   son _____

eight _____   tow _____

tale _____   hair _____

Homophones

Name _____

1. **Write the word that matches the picture.**

a. flour   flower

_____

b. pear   pair

_____

c. some   sum

$$4 + 6$$
$$= 10$$

_____

d. dear   deer

_____

e. rain   rein

_____

f. mail   male

_____

2. **Choose the correct word and complete each sentence.**

a. It is rude to _____ at others. (**stair   stare**)

b. I ate a large piece of _____ for lunch. (**stake   steak**)

c. His hands were _____ behind his back with thick rope. (**tide   tied**)

d. When she kicked the ball she hurt her _____. (**toe   tow**)

e. The man felt _____ after the long operation. (**week   weak**)

3. **Can you spot three pairs of homophones in the box? Write them on the lines in pairs.**

pearwringmalepairmailring

_____   _____   _____

_____   _____   _____

From Time-Savers for Teachers: Spelling Years 3-4. This page may be reproduced for classroom use.

81

Homophones

Name _____

Choose the correct word to complete each sentence.

1. **a.** The baby began to _____ when Paul took her toy. (**bawl ball**)

   b. Have you ever _____ to Spain? (**bean been**)

   c. The wind _____ strongly all night long. (**blew blue**)

   d. A _____ is like a large rabbit. (**hare hair**)

   e. The anchored _____ showed the yachts the deepest water. (**buoys boys**)

2. **a.** The _____ and its fawn were in the forest. (**deer dear**)

   b. I am going to _____ my hair black. (**dye die**)

   c. Asha _____ a strange noise in the room. (**heard herd**)

   d. The bus conductor took my _____. (**fair fare**)

   e. Some animals have thick _____ to keep them warm. (**fir fur**)

3. **a.** The _____ made the dog scratch. (**flea flee**)

   b. A rose is a beautiful _____. (**flower flour**)

   c. There are sixty minutes in one _____. (**our hour**)

   d. Ravi _____ the answers to all the questions. (**knew new**)

   e. Joanne tied a _____ in the string. (**knot not**)

4. **a.** This table is _____ of wood. (**maid made**)

   b. Henry began to _____ through the curtains. (**peer pier**)

   c. The teacher is going to _____ us a story. (**reed read**)

   d. The headmaster asked Josh to _____ the bell. (**wring ring**)

   e. The farmer began to _____ the wheat. (**sow sew**)

Homophones

Name _____

Choose the correct word to complete each sentence.

1. **a.** We _____ like to know when they will arrive. (wood would)

    b. The clothes in this shop are quite _____. (cheap cheep)

    c. We caught _____ fish in the lake. (two too)

    d. The greedy girl ate the _____ cake. (hole whole)

    e. Are you going to come _____? (in inn)

2. **a.** Yesterday Anita _____ a book about snakes. (red read)

    b. It was dark and stormy last _____. (night knight)

    c. I ate a juicy _____. (pear pair)

    d. I would like another _____ of cake please. (piece peace)

    e. This cake is made from _____ flour. (plane plain)

3. **a.** We had to _____ the blinds to see outside. (rays raise)

    b. The cowboy _____ his horse into the town. (rode road)

    c. We go to church to _____. (prey pray)

    d. I am going to _____ the tea into the cup. (poor pour)

    e. We have a lot of _____ during winter. (rain rein)

4. **In the grid find a homophone for each word. Write them on the lines.**

d	e	a	r	w	o	o	d
f	t	h	b	r	o	a	r
l	i	a	l	r	o	s	e
e	e	i	e	p	o	o	r
a	d	r	w	p	r	a	y
w	e	e	k	f	a	r	e

tide _____   deer _____

would _____   blue _____

prey _____   raw _____

rows _____   flee _____

hare _____   pour _____

fair _____   weak _____

Homophones

Name _____

1. Write each word beside its homophone. The first one has been done for you.

ball	been	road	wood
week	their	tee	rein

a. bawl   **ball**   e. rain   _____

b. rode   _____   f. tea   _____

c. there   _____   g. weak   _____

d. would   _____   h. bean   _____

2. Write each word beside its homophone. The first one has been done for you.

ate	new	blue	flower
saw	two	steel	sail

a. eight   **ate**   b. blew   _____   c. sore   _____

d. steal   _____   e. flour   _____   f. sale   _____

g. knew   _____   h. too   _____

3. Circle the word with the same letter string.

a. **nine** – paper pine chair   e. **room** – broom carpet bench

b. **life** – knife pin most   f. **cake** – eat sponge lake

c. **house** – table apple mouse   g. **river** – shiver orange gold

d. **boat** – ship coat over   h. **bone** – seven cone never

Answers to Homophones

Answers to page 79

sun, toe, two, see, eight, hare, rose, pear, sail, tail, mail, knot, flour, deer, rain, sum, pair, bean, plane, wood

Answers to page 80

1 sun, toe, two, eight, sail, hare

2 hour, fur, sea, tale, flee

3 not, see, ate, tail, two or to, sun, toe, hare

Answers to page 81

1 flower, pear, sum, deer, rain, male

2 stare, steak, tied, toe, weak

3
pear, pair;
wring, ring;
male, mail

Answers to page 82

1 bawl, been, blew, hare, buoys

2 deer, dye, heard, fare, fur

3 flea, flower, hour, knew, knot

4 made, peer, read, ring, sow

Answers to page 83

1 would, cheap, two, whole, in

2 read, night, pear, piece, plain

3 raise, rode, pray, pour, rain

4 tied, wood, pray, rose, hair, fare, dear, blew, roar, flea, poor, week

Answers to page 84

1 road, their, wood, rein, tee, week, been

2 steel, new, blue, flower, two, saw, sail

3 pine, knife, mouse, coat, broom, lake, shiver, cone

Introduction to Spelling Practice

The 'Spelling strategies' section for Years 3 and 4 of Word level work in the National Literacy Strategy lists all the techniques that pupils can use to improve their spelling knowledge:

- sounding out and spelling and using phonemes;

- using visual skills, e.g. recognising common letter strings and checking critical features (i.e. does it look right, shape, length, etc?);

- building from other words with similar patterns and meanings, e.g. medical, medicine;

- spelling by analogy with other known words, e.g. light, fright;

- using word banks, dictionaries;

- practising new spellings regularly by 'look, say, cover, write, check' strategy.

This final section of worksheets should therefore help pupils to distinguish and discriminate between right and wrong spellings, and help them to proofread their own work for accuracy.

Spelling Practice

Name _____

1. Circle each correct word.

   a. night   nite   **b.** craem   cream   **c.** aple   apple

   d. baby   babby   **e.** buter   butter   **f.** sixty   sixtey

   g. yelow   yellow   **h.** litle   little

2. Add the missing letter to each word.

   a. ri___er   **b.** ho___se   **c.** c___ke

   d. b___tter   **e.** w___ndow   **f.** sw___ng

   g. t___nt   **h.** p___nd    **i.** ro___nd

3. Find words in the grid. Match each to its picture.

n	e	s	t	d
r	a	i	n	r
f	o	o	t	u
w	o	o	d	m
b	a	b	y	x

a. _____   **b.** _____

c. _____   **d.** _____

e. _____

Spelling Practice

Name _____

1. **Circle the correct spelling of each word.**

   a. pilow   pillow   **b.** about   abuot   **c.** begin   beggin

   d. light   lite   **e.** papper   paper   **f.** sumer   summer

   g. shu   shoe   **h.** water   watter   **i.** stone   stoan

2. **The words in the two boxes can be linked. Write them together here.**

   e.g.   every + day = everyday

light	bull	black	dust
place	court	spring	shoe

   _____   _____

   _____   _____

bird	house	dog	storm
mat	yard	time	lace

   _____   _____

   _____   _____

3. **In the grid find as many words as you can. There are sixteen.**

t	r	u	c	k	h	b	c	b
w	w	s	s	h	i	u	o	i
a	o	o	a	a	d	l	l	r
s	r	a	i	i	e	l	d	d
h	d	p	d	r	f	a	l	l
d	u	c	k	g	l	a	s	s
f	a	s	t	p	o	n	y	x
k	i	l	l	e	d	x	x	x

   _____   _____

   _____   _____

   _____   _____

   _____   _____

   _____   _____

   _____   _____

   _____   _____

   _____   _____

Spelling Practice

Name _____

1. **Incorrect homophones have been used below. Write the passage again using the correct words.**

   One day when the <u>son</u> was shining brightly I <u>sore</u> a large ship with a bright <u>read</u> <u>sale</u> on the <u>see</u>. The sky was <u>blew</u> and I could <u>here</u> the sound of some <u>buoys</u> bouncing a <u>bawl</u> on the <u>peer</u>.

   _____

   _____

   _____

   _____

   _____

2. **In each sentence circle the correct spelling.**

   a. I like to put (**creem cream**) on my strawberries.

   b. The weather was stormy last (**night nite**).

   c. Sally is big but Mo is (**little littel**).

   d. Tom is a boy but Ling is a (**girl gril**).

   e. It sometimes snows during the (**wintar winter**) months.

   f. Jack fell (**doun down**) the well.

3. **There are six spelling mistakes in this story. Underline each one and then write it correctly.**

   I ate an aple for my dinner tooday. I like to eat lotz of food eech day becorse it keaps me healthy.

   _____   _____   _____

   _____   _____   _____

From Time-Savers for Teachers: Spelling Years 3-4. This page may be reproduced for classroom use.

89

Spelling Practice

Name _____

1. **Read the passage then write the correct word in each space.**

    One dark ᵃ_____ a ᵇ_____ put on his ᶜ_____
    and went outside to milk the cows. As he walked ᵈ_____ the path
    a large ᵉ_____ flew above his ᶠ_____.

    a. nite night   **b.** farmer farmar   **c.** cote coat

    d. down dorn   **e.** brid bird   **f.** hed head

2. **Find and correct all the errors below. Write the whole passage underneath.**

    I lik to go to bed rite afta I have wached my favourite television serie.
    If I wont to stay up later I have to arsk my muther. Once she siad that I
    culd watch more television if I worked harder at skool.

    _____

    _____

    _____

    _____

    _____

3. **Circle the correct spelling of each word.**

    a. Last night I had a (dreem dream) about snakes.

    b. I like to spread (buter butter) on my bread.

    c. The dog ate a juicy (bown bone).

    d. I ate a small cream (cake cak) for my lunch.

    e. It is over a (week weeck) since I have seen him.

    f. This shape is called a (sqare square).

Spelling Practice

Name _____

1. **Circle the correct spelling of the word in brackets.**

   a.   An elephant is big but a mouse is (littel **little**).

   b.   Mike is a very (**quick** quik) runner.

   c.   At the zoo we saw a large (loin **lion**).

   d.   This rock is heavy but this paper is (lite **light**).

   e.   The baby put the food in its (muoth **mouth**).

   f.   A (rabit **rabbit**) lives in a burrow.

2. **The incorrect homophones have been used below. Rewrite the passage using the correct words.**

   The cowboy <u>tide</u> his <u>hoarse</u> to the <u>steak</u> and went inside the shop to <u>by</u> <u>sum cheep</u> food. When he returned he jumped on his horse, grabbed the <u>rains</u>, and <u>road</u> towards the <u>heard</u> of cattle that had <u>bean</u> waiting for him on the <u>plane</u>.

   _____

   _____

   _____

   _____

   _____

3. **Find all eight words spelled incorrectly in this passage. Write them correctly on the lines.**

   The wite rabit was running acros a feild when it saw a kiten. It stoped and went bak and saw that it was eating a muose.

   _____   _____   _____   _____

   _____   _____   _____   _____

From Time-Savers for Teachers: Spelling Years 3-4. This page may be reproduced for classroom use.

91

Spelling Practice

Name _____

1. **Choose the correct spelling of the word to fill each space.**

   One day a tiger went to the ^a_____ to get a drink of
   ^b_____. As it was drinking it saw a ^c_____ swimming
   ^d_____ it. The tiger decided to ^e_____ because it
   ^f_____ sense the danger.

a. river rivver	**b.** warter water	**c.** crokadile crocodile
d. toowards towards	**e.** leave leeve	**f.** could culd

2. **Rewrite each sentence, correcting any spelling or grammar errors.**

   a. My muther drives a large truk.

   _____

   b. The conducter gave me a tiket.

   _____

   c. There was not meny lollies left in the paket.

   _____

   d. She told us there was fourty ducks eating the brerd.

   _____

   e. The papper plane flew over the huose.

   _____

   f. We walk to skool evry day of the week.

   _____

3. **Look at each group of words. Circle the correct spelling.**

a. aple appel apple		**e.** markit market marcket
b. pilow pillow pillo		**f.** because bekause becorse
c. every evry evary		**g.** bottel bottle botel
d. summer sumer summa		**h.** nife knife kniffe

Spelling Practice

Name _____

1. **Choose the correct spelling of each word and complete each sentence.**

   a. Shaheen is _____ first at school. (allways always)

   b. Lucas _____ he would help us later. (said siad)

   c. Joanne came last and Mo came _____ in the race. (first frist)

   d. I hope to become a _____ when I leave school. (docter doctor)

   e. It is _____ past seven o'clock. (allready already)

   f. An elephant is a very large _____. (aminal animal)

2. **These eight words have been squashed together. Use each one to complete a sentence.**

   > offuntildoesshoesbecauseloseboughtopen

   a. This door is shut but that one is _____.

   b. The girl jumped _____ the table and onto the floor.

   c. We must wait here _____ the rain stops.

   d. Joanne is wearing a new pair of leather _____.

   e. Chris cannot come out to play _____ he is ill.

   f. My father _____ me a new jumper.

   g. Be careful you don't _____ your way in the forest.

   h. He always _____ his homework as soon as he arrives home.

3. **Circle the correct spelling of each word.**

   a. could   culd   **e.** allways   always

   b. write   rite   **f.** ask   arsk

   c. suger   sugar   **g.** because   becorse

   d. untill   until   **h.** skool   school

Answers to Spelling Practice

Answers to page 87

1 night, cream, apple, baby, butter, sixty, yellow, little

2 river, horse, cake, butter, window, swing, tent, pond, round

3 baby, rain, foot, drum, nest

Answers to page 88

1 pillow, about, begin, light, paper, summer, shoe, water, stone

2 lighthouse, bulldog, blackbird, duststorm, placemat, courtyard, springtime, shoelace

3 answers include: truck, fall, duck, glass, fast, pony, killed, wash, word, soap, said, hair, hide, bull, cold, bird

Answers to page 89

1 One day when the sun was shining brightly I saw a large ship with a bright red sail on the sea. The sky was blue and I could hear the sounds of some boys bouncing a ball on the pier.

2 cream, night, little, girl, winter, down

3 apple, today, lots, each, because, keeps

Answers to page 90

1 night, farmer, coat, down, bird, head

2 I like to go to bed right after I have watched my favourite television series. If I want to stay up later I have to ask my mother. Once she said that I could watch more television if I worked harder at school.

3 dream, butter, bone, cake, week, square

Answers to page 91

1 little, quick, lion, light, mouth, rabbit

2 tied, horse, stake, buy, some, cheap, reins, rode, herd, been, plain

3 white, rabbit, across, field, kitten, stopped, back, mouse

Answers to page 92

1 river, water, crocodile, towards, leave, could

2

a My mother drives a large truck.

b The conductor gave me a ticket.

c There were not many lollies left in the packet.

d She told us there were forty ducks eating the bread.

e The paper plane flew over the house.

f We walk to school every day of the week.

3 apple, pillow, every, summer, market, because, bottle, knife

Answers to page 93

1 always, said, first, doctor, already, animal

2 open, off, until, shoes, because, bought, lose, does

3 could, write, sugar, until, always, ask, because, school

Index